MW00653181

REAL WOMEN

Adventures in Sisterhood

by
Sandra J. Gooselaw

PublishAmerica
Baltimore

First printing

At the specific preference of the author, PublishAmerica allowed this work to remain exactly as the author intended, verbatim, without editorial input.

ISBN: 1-4241-1959-6
PUBLISHED BY PUBLISHAMERICA, LLLP
www.publishamerica.com
Baltimore

Printed in the United States of America

This book is dedicated
With deepest love and affection
To my husband, Phil and our
four children, Kym, Jason, Min and Tahnya

ACKNOWLEDGMENTS

My heartfelt appreciation to PublishAmerica for believing in me and my project. Thank you to Danielle McDonald, my first contact at PublishAmerica, for your friendly and welcoming spirit.

A HUGE, HUGE thank you to my dear friend Carla who read the first chapter of my book last fall and believed in my vision. And for the next several months committed herself to reading a new chapter every week, and sending it back in the mail with words of encouragement written all over the pages. Truly, without her strong belief in my dream for this book, it would not be a reality today. You are always in my balcony with your clear voice and bright light shining on me.

To my husband and *best friend* Phil, who has always believed in me and surrounded me with his love, support and constant encouragement. You have taught me to live authentically and to give the world the best part of myself. You light up my life.

To the two most incredible people who gave me my start in life, my mom and dad, who allowed me to be myself growing up, never putting boundaries on my spirit and creativity. Who gave me wings and let me soar.

To my friend Jill Hallgren who has and continues to fill my mailbox with her creative writing over these past few years keeping me constantly inspired.

To my friend Nancy Marsh, who was always willing to share her writing wisdom with me and being available at a moments notice when I needed advice.

And to my friends who have gone before me, and to those still walking this journey of "Sisterhood" beside me, allowing me to share their stories in my book. And to those friends whose personal stories are not found in my book. If you read carefully you will find pieces of yourselves among these stories.

To my four beautiful children, Min, Kym, Tahnya, and Jason who gave me the special privilege of being their mom.

To God, for this exceptional life He has given me.

INTRODUCTION

A few nights ago I sat in our library in front of a crackling fire with a mug of hot chocolate piled high with whipped cream and the new February 2004 issue of Ladies Home Journal. Earlier, at the grocery store, I passed the magazine stand and spotted Diane Sawyer's picture on the cover of LHJ. So I grabbed a copy and tossed it in my cart. Later that evening, as I curled up in front of the fire, I began reading about this TV celebrity who seems so real. I knew she had to be pretty perfect, at least that's what we assume about people we don't know. I started reading about her fears that she shared so easily with her interviewer. I'm thinking she wouldn't have to admit these fears. Who would know? Her honesty really caught my attention. Then when asked, "What is your favorite thing you and your husband do when you aren't working?" I was surprised when she answered, "Curl up at home and watch movies or have a quiet dinner together with good conversation." HMMM...There went my dream of vicariously living a dream date with Diane Sawyer and her husband.

As the interview progressed her interviewer commented on her socks. "Oh, these are my husband's socks". So here's a lady with the ability to dress with the latest fashions and she's wearing her husband's socks at a magazine interview. The crackling of the fire p u l l e d my attention away from Diane's article and I sat there watching the flames dancing up and down the logs. As the warmth from the fire embraced my body, I realized the candid, honest replies of Diane's interview were equally "warming my soul". I finished the article and pulled the quilt that was hanging over the back of the couch up around me and started thinking about how often we want to present ourselves, our lives, as perfect, but how freeing it would be if we lost all the pretension and became real.

Do you suppose Diane wore those socks just to make the interviewer comfortable as she was interviewing this very successful woman? Or, maybe, Diane was just being *real.*

What I have noticed in conversations with many friends this past year that is always the same, they want friends who are authentic and real. They are tired of the pretension that often overshadows friendship. They are tired of the competition, false relationships and gossip that often fill daily conversations. They want to surround themselves with friendships that are honest and genuine. Being real is showing the humanness we all possess if we let our guard down and dare to be real. As women, we are impacted and inspired by positive women and how they live their lives.

I have always wanted to write a book about women with amazing spirits, but the time never seemed right or the stories weren't there. ('The truth is "we all have amazing spirits" and, we all have stories to tell.) In 2003 I lost two of my closest friends to cancer. Each of their journeys was different. I was blessed to share these incredible journeys with my friends. Sitting by the fire reading Diane's story and realizing how touched I was by her candidness, it all of a sudden seemed so clear to me that this was the time to begin writing my book. The stories are here.

I invite you now to join me on my journey with amazing women who have graced my life as I share their courageous and real stories of life and friendship with you.

Blessings,

Sandy Gooselaw

SISTERHOOD

I was sitting with one of my sisters-in-law at a restaurant a few days ago and she looked at me and said, "We need to give time to our sisters in the midst of our busy lives." I think she thought I might have been daydreaming because she repeated it and said, "We really do!" She went on to say, "Sisters are not just the women in our family, but are also the women who pass through our lives who become our sisters." I think what she was trying to say to me was that we often let life keep us so distracted by busyness, that we give second-place to what is really valuable in life. As I drove home later that afternoon I found myself thinking about all the sisters who have found a home in my heart, and how empty my life would be without them. I also thought about the friendships that haven't worked, and wondered why? Have you ever had a friend that you really like for so many reasons, but then for as many other reasons there is way too much work that goes into making that friendship feel good? Or a friend that reels you in and just when you think this friendship is going somewhere they let out the line or cut the line. And the thing is, you know in your heart somewhere down the line they're going to reel you in again. And somehow, we keep falling for the bait that draws us in, until one day we realize "we" need to be the one cutting the line. All friendships aren't meant to survive, but when they do, we know it, because they develop without effort. They're like resting on a soft, fluffy pillow.

These sisters come in all shapes and sizes, and we try them on like a pair of shoes at the mall. Some fit perfectly and others pinch our toes. Not all acquaintances are meant to stay for a lifetime. Some come to visit for a while and then move on. Friendship should be easy and not something that feels like a full-time job to us. I grew up in a family with five brothers, and no biological sisters. But on my journey through life I have acquired many sisters that began as friendship. And I have found they show up in the least expected ways. One showed up at my front door on a rainy afternoon as a client, and now we're sisters in friendship. I find these unexpected friends become invaluable treasures that I cherish.

I love sharing in conversations with women when you go beyond the normal day-to-day chitchat. In some friendships it never goes beyond the chitchat, but in others you rarely spend time in small talk. This past week our niece visited us from Minnesota. She is 25 years old. One evening after dinner I asked her if she wanted to watch a movie. She said, "Let's go look at family albums." So we went down to our library, put a log on the fire, (even though it was the middle of summer- I wanted to create a little atmosphere), and spent about five minutes looking at pictures. And then the most amazing thing happened. We started talking about our dreams, our fears, sharing life experiences. When we finally looked at the clock it was 4 a.m. We had been talking all night. Because we live so far away from each other we had never had these conversations before. We bonded that night as we sat in front of a crackling fire, daring to share our failures, embracing our accomplishments, celebrating our possibilities as women.

When we dream together, support and encourage each other, we help each other to succeed in life. We all have dreams, but dreams are usually accompanied by fear.

When I do my creative writing I often sit at a window upstairs in our guest room overlooking Mount Pilchuck. I like looking at the mountain as I write, because it reminds me that my writing projects are like climbing that mountain. When I begin a new project it looms before me like an impossible task. Just like standing at the base of that mountain looking up and thinking about climbing it, makes it feel impossible. But we know if we just take one small step at a time we will eventually reach the top. With writing it begins the same way, with just one word at a time. We rarely achieve anything without fear, but *despite our fears*. We succeed because we walk through our fears. Our imagination is skilled at inhabiting the negative. It's easier to see the negative and talk ourselves out of the new adventure we had dreamed of embarking on. Try embracing optimism. Picture yourself living smack in the middle of your wildest dreams.

As my niece and I said goodnight through blurred vision and deep yawns, we each took a gift to bed with us that night of connecting in our hearts in "sisterhood".

I believe when we open ourselves up to each other with our stories, we give our sisters encouragement. We realize we are not the *only one* having this unique experience, whatever that experience might be. That no ones' life is perfect, even though they appear that way to us sometimes. We all share the same fears. If we could step out of our insecurities, most of us would choose to be real with each other. Perfection is not only an illusion, but also a lot of work trying to attain it and few women can relate to it.

13

CARLA

Life has a way of bringing us gifts in the midst of ordinary days.

About four years ago I was working in my office one morning when my phone rang. As I answered it there was a client on the other end wanting to make an appointment for later that afternoon. My schedule was full and I told her I wouldn't be able to see her. We continued talking and before I knew it she had an appointment to see me at two. Isn't it funny how that happens? Those appointments always end up being a "gift" in my day. I was with a client when Carla arrived at my door at 2pm. I let her in and showed her into my living room. It had been a full day and I was looking forward to wrapping up my days work. I finished with my client and let her out, then walked into my living room to invite my new client into my office. For some reason I sat down on a couch across from her and asked how her day was going. Two hours later we went into my office.

When I opened my front door to Carla that afternoon I realized right away there was something special about

15

her. The warmth in her voice when she said hello, the sincerity I felt in just the first few words we exchanged. In those two hours we shared life stories. Things you only share with the closest of friends. When she left that day I knew I had just made a new friend. Sometimes when we try to close doors, for some reason they stay open. I call these special events, serendipity. I call these special friends, diamonds. Diamonds are those friends that are real. They say things how they are without editing to sugar coat and present themselves in a perfect light. They share their humanness with you and invite you to be human with them. They dare to trust you with their stories. One day if we're lucky we end up with a diamond necklace.

Several years ago my husband was listening to a conversation I was having with a friend on the phone. When I hung up he asked me "Why do you always do that?" "Do what?" I asked. When you talk to, we'll call her Suzy, you never talk real. Everything is always perfect to both of you. Life isn't like that. Are you ever honest with each other? As I thought about what he said later that night, I thought, he's right. Neither one of us let our guard down to say how it really is. We both did have good lives and we were happy, but no matter how good life is, nothing is perfect. And we both painted a perfect world to each other. And the result was our friendship was shallow, even though we were good friends and had been friends since our children were babies. I thought a lot about what my husband said that day. I appreciated my friends that came to me to share a difficult situation and trusted me with that information. As I continued to think about how real I was, I started analyzing myself. I was blessed with this positive, happy spirit. I enjoyed life and had a passion for living. I enjoyed every day and just believed that sometimes there are days that are harder than others. I wasn't a complainer and truly was thankful for the life I was given. But I was beginning to realize I wasn't always real with my friends. And so I began working on being real.

And what I immediately realized was that my friendships deepened and the new friends I attracted were more genuine.

Carla was one of those new friends. Carla's elegant and classy and has a natural beauty. She is always 100% present when you are with her. She speaks from her heart and listens with her soul. Like my friend Ruthie, she has a love for scarves! Carla can make blue jeans and a sweater look classy by just tossing a colorful scarf over her shoulder or draping one around her neck. She has choppy blond hair and a big beautiful smile. Her zest for life is contagious.

Energy flows from her voice when she speaks and she has an easy laugh. Carla inhales life! And she is so real. She opens the door for you to be real. What a gift she brings to the world. Our phone conversations that sometimes go on for hours nurture my soul. We dissect life together and marvel at all the opportunities it offers us. We talk about dreams, disappointments, what ifs, quiet picnics on lazy salt-water beaches away from fast food and freeway traffic jams. We muse over what part of ourselves we want to leave in this world. How can we make it a better place while we're here?

Carla dares to step out of the box. She gets an idea and runs with it. Her spirit is full of adventure. She's wise and intuitive. What I love most about my friend—she's real!

RUTHIE'S STORY

I had just come home from an afternoon of errands. As I passed the answer machine the message light was blinking. I hit the button and heard my friend Ruthie's voice inviting me to meet her at Starbuck's later that night for a latte. Driving there that night I wondered if she had something special to share with me or if she just wanted to hang out and chat. I pulled into Starbucks next to her car and saw she was already there. I walked through the door excited about having this special time with my friend after a busy day. I looked around for Ruthie and there she was, way back at a corner table. She motioned for me to join her.

I had only met Ruthie 6 months earlier. A friend introduced us at church. A month later she invited my husband and I along with some other friends to their home. We hit it off that first night and quickly developed a special bond.

As I walked into her beautiful home that night, I realized we had two obvious things in common. We both loved to decorate (taupe & cream) :) and we both loved clothes. What else do you need to form a deep friendship?

My new friend was physically beautiful, but as I began to know her I saw this genuine, warm inner spirit that complimented her outer beauty.

I joined Ruthie and we began talking about the events of our day and then she looked at me and took my hands in hers and said, "I have something to tell you." My first thought was, "She's having a menopause baby". She was happy and healthy. What else could it be?

Then she said those words that we never want to hear and when we do hear them, we always think that somehow we misunderstood what was just said to us. With bravery and an uncanny calm she said, "I have breast cancer". The next two hours were a blur. We held each other and cried. We talked and even found things to laugh about. Isn't that what you do when all of a sudden the world doesn't make sense anymore? You find something to laugh about? Those three words took our perfect lives and changed everything. The world didn't feel the same. Life didn't feel the same.

About 10:30 we realized our surroundings had grown quiet and as we looked towards the front of the store two employees stood behind the counter looking at us. As we stood up and apologized for staying so late, (they closed at 10pm!) they encouraged us to stay longer if we needed to. We thanked them for their sensitive spirit with us and each headed to our own car. As I hugged my friend good-bye I didn't want to let go of her. We both drove to our homes in surreal worlds that night.

This journey with Ruthie lasted the next four years. I

watched my friend go through a double mastectomy, chemo, lose her hair, lose her spirit at times, lose weight, gain weight, sleep for days, cry, but through it all, be incredibly brave. In the fall of 2003, I was spending the night with our oldest son's girlfriend and at 7am my husband called and said Ruthie had just been taken to the hospital. They were doing surgery the following morning. Later that day I drove to the hospital and asked the staff if I could spend the night with my friend so her husband could go home and rest before the next day. They made up a bed for me beside her bed and again I felt like I was in a "special place" having this "slumber party" with her. God places us in these exceptional places and moments and they compare to nothing in the real world. As we lay side by side in this dark hospital room we talked of things we don't talk about in the daylight of our homes and ordinary lives. These moments are "extraordinary gifts." We almost lost Ruthie after that surgery, but somewhere in her spirit she knew it wasn't time to go yet. She was probably ready, but I think she knew the rest of us weren't. When she returned home she needed daily care and supervision while her husband went to work. A group of us signed up to each take a day of the week. Each week I looked forward to this time with Ruthie. In this last year I watched her life regain some normalcy. We went shopping, out to lunch, took long strolls around the farm, we shared our life stories with each other and our conversations often led to what lay ahead for her. She wasn't afraid to talk about dying. But I noticed one thing about our conversations. She was always in a little different place than I was. She was seeing the world a little brighter than I did. She was noticing all the details. She was collecting memories to take with her.

When I was in Ruthie's presence I knew there were always three of us present, because she always kept God close beside her. In every conversation we shared there were three subjects that we never missed talking about. Her love for her husband Ernie, her children and God. In many of our strolls around the farm I'd be talking to my friend and she'd be talking out loud to God. And I just knew she was in a more important place.

Ruthie spent this last year preparing all of us for the last part of her journey and in November she said good-bye.

As we go through life we collect all different kinds of friends and every once in awhile we are given a friend who stands out from all the rest. I call them diamonds. Ruthie was one of my diamonds. I have always felt that it is such an honor to be in the presence of someone as they are preparing to leave this world. They see things so much brighter than the rest of us and they see details that we often miss. One afternoon in the summer of her final year, Ruthie and I were having lunch on her patio and I was in my bare feet. Ruthie put her fork down and looked at me and said, "Let's go walking barefoot in the grass". She kicked off her shoes and we went walking all over the field and talked about the grass tickling our feet. Something the rest of us might so easily have missed. She took me across the field and recalled a memory of a special tree their family had planted there many years ago. I stood there watching my friend embracing life and saying good-bye to memories.

What will I always remember about my friend? When she entered a room her presence commanded everyone's attention. She had a genuine love for people and had a gift of making anyone in her presence feel loved and unique. She shared her love without reservation. Everything about my friend spoke of *class*. Ruthie had an amazing spirit!

PAM

Pam has the gift of being an exceptional mom and I rarely see her without a child clinging to each leg and a baby resting on her hip. Pam is patient. She can quiet a noisy room without raising her voice. Pam has a heart for kids and has added two adopted children to her family of three biological children. When you enter her home there is a sense of peace and calm. There is an orderliness that rarely is seen in such a big family.

I never see dirty dishes in her sink. Where do you suppose she puts them?? She is never harried and portrays the same peace that fills her home. She is always showered and dressed at daybreak. When does she sleep??

Pam is a talented decorator and we share this love for decorating our homes. Her home is filled with bright yellows, brilliant blues and purples and splashes of red in unsuspecting places.

Pam is the Martha Stewart of our neighborhood. You don't want to stand still too long in her presence because she paints anything that is stationary. She carries a paintbrush in her hip pocket and is, at a moments notice, prepared to paint. She loves perusing the local antique stores bringing home lifeless pieces and turning them into sought after collectibles by her friends. Doorless kitchen cupboards burst with colorful dishes and glassware. Bright colored shutters grace her windowsills and frame archways.

A milk bench displays plates and glasses on her kitchen counter. Pam dares to step out of the box when it comes to decorating.

What do I love about Pam? She is so real. She's easy and fun to be around. She's honest and forthright.

She doesn't let you get away with anything. She reads your thoughts and knows what you're thinking. She seeks out the truth in what you're really trying to say and removes all the fancy wrapping we use when trying to disguise our true thoughts.

She doesn't allow for pretension in her midst.

She is real and she wants those around her to be the same way. She doesn't paint perfect pictures of her life. And she expects you to use the same honesty with her.

Our friendship is usually energized by our decorating forays. One of us always has a project going or a new idea with an urgency to be shared. But every once in awhile we stop and sit down in her kitchen when the house is quiet and everyone is gone and we talk about life. That's when I really get to know my friend. I cherish those times and tuck them away in my memory.

What have I learned from my friend Pam? That when life takes us on paths we hadn't planned on traveling, you just adjust your sails. Some things we can't change. We just adjust the way we look at it.

You know the story about the orange. You squeeze an orange and what do you get? Orange Juice! When you squeeze a person what do you get? What is truly inside of them. I have seen my friend squeezed and what comes out is always the same. Just like the orange. Orange juice!

But what I really want to know is "Where are those dirty dishes??"

LINDA

What a journey life takes us on sometimes. But the gift of any journey is the memories we collect along the way. Now as I look back over the past 30 years of our friendship these are some of **"my favorite memories."**

The stormy nights when our lights would go out and she'd come over and stay in our guest room. We'd cook soup on the wood stove and eat by candlelight. There was always something a little eerie as we listened to the wind howling outside and the creaking of the big evergreen trees in the front yard. After dinner we'd all grab a quilt and snuggle up close to the warm, crackling fire telling stories and laughing together. Those were special nights for all of us.

The morning her son Jeff came over when she had spent the night and we all ate waffles together.

The many years of gathering on New Years day at her home, eating her famous lasagna and watching our toddlers grow into young people.

Our walks and long talks on the Centennial Trail.

Sharing her cozy Coupeville cabin with us. The cabin was so much like Linda. Unpretentious, cozy and comfortable with its natural planked walls, big stone fireplace in the living room and windows everywhere to view the water and mountains. And if we were lucky an eagle would gracefully fly close by just to add to the already perfect atmosphere. It was a place to quiet your spirit and refresh your soul.

We all have a friend that we look at with admiration and appreciation for qualities that make them unique and are an inspiration in our own life. God blessed her with this **"Huge Heart"** that was full of caring and love for people of all walks of life and He blessed her with this awesome gift of **humility**.

I was sitting by the fire and quilting one night and just enjoying all the bright fabrics I was sewing with and thinking how friendships are a lot like the different textures and colorful fabrics. Some fabrics are bold and bright and that reminds me of friends that are energizing to me. Striped fabrics represent the many different qualities in our friends. And then there are the pastel colors that represent our quiet, peaceful friends. They're like a stream of calm water flowing through our lives. Linda was my stream of calm water. Always steady, always flowing smoothly.

She left an awesome legacy as a mom to her children, of someone who has helped to make our world a better place to live, just because she was here, teaching and caring for all of us.

She was an example to each one of us with the way she

handled this challenge with so much dignity and grace. You know they say, "It's easy to look good when everything is going O.K., but our true character comes out when our world is turned upside down. One of my favorite sayings goes: "We cannot direct the wind, but we can adjust the sails."

This **"wind"** rocked her world for 10 years and as we all watched her continually adjusting her sails we saw only strength and calm. In the midst of this storm that was ever present in her life, she found peace. She was the one who gave each of us the strength to walk this journey with her and to let her go when the time came. I remember the night she called last November to say it was time to begin saying our good-byes. There's a funny thing that happens with extended illness. I fooled myself into believing she was always going to be here. Because she always got back up. There's also something beautiful that happens when we come to this place in our life. If given the time and opportunity, we begin to say things that often go unsaid. Her call that night was a gift of opportunity. We stayed on the phone a long time that night. Like my friend Ruthie, Linda hung around a lot longer than she probably wanted to, but she made sure we all had plenty of time to say good-bye. Linda stayed with us 2 ½ months after that November phone call. I remember having to schedule appointments to see her each week because her days were so full of friends gathering to visit with her, *just one more time.*

After that November phone call from her doctor, Linda did an amazing thing. She invited a handful of her friends and her children over on a Sunday afternoon. She asked us all to help her plan her "Life Celebration

Service". She did it with a smile on her face and an air of poise and confidence. In the midst of the planning there was even joking and laughing. She had one request — that it be happy. She taught her kids that day that death is OK to talk about and that there are things in life that we sometimes just can't change. She taught us all that day to be brave in the midst of our challenges. To step up in the face of fear and accept what we can't change and to make every moment exceptional.

As we gathered around her that day we didn't know it, but we had already begun her "Celebration of Life." And that day was truly exceptional.

She left a rich legacy to all of us who knew her of "what the important things in life are." No matter how hard I looked at my friend's life, I could only see one thing that mattered to her. "**People.**" Her family and friends. She always let us know how important each of us was to her.

I met my friend Linda 30 years ago when we both adopted our first babies from Korea. She went on to adopt 4 more children. In the midst of raising 5 children she went back to college and graduated with a Psychology degree and then began her teaching career.

Linda had a soft, gentle spirit and a strength that never swayed. One year for my birthday she gave me a framed poem that read, **"Some people come into our life, and quietly go, others leave footprints on our hearts that remain forever"**. My friend left footprints on my heart. She was an angel in my life. Everyone she met walked away with her "footprints" on their heart. Linda truly embraced all that life gave her and freely shared the *best of herself* with the world.

INGE

It was the fall of 1988 and I was in San Francisco marketing my book that had just arrived from the publisher. I had a   booth at the Trade Center on Mission Street where store buyers came from all over the world to buy items for their stores. Sellers purchase a booth for four days and then market their products. The days were filled with excitement. By the fourth day I was tired and ready to pack up my things and head to the airport to catch my plane home. Most of the buyers had already left town with their purchases. There are guidelines when you purchase a booth, and one of the guidelines was that you work your booth for three full days, and the morning of the fourth day. On the last day the center closed at noon.

When I arrived at the center on the fourth day, most of the sellers were busy packing up their products. The place was quiet with only a few straggling buyers wandering the aisles. Many of the sellers had already vacated their booths. When I arrived at my booth my neighbor leaned around the curtain that separated our booths and said "this lady has been to your booth several times this morning and keeps asking when you were coming in." I began filling boxes with my books and wondering, "Who was this lady?" It wasn't long before she was standing in front of me. Remember the diamonds I talked about in an earlier story? Inge became another one of those diamonds.

Inge is 5 feet 9 inches tall, slender, with steel gray hair and blazing blue eyes that dance with mischief. Inge is beautiful. In the following couple of hours Inge and I became friends and her parting words were "let's do lunch." That year notes passed back and forth between our mailboxes and we had long visits on the phone. A friendship was growing. A year later my phone rang one morning and it was Inge calling from San Francisco saying, "Let's do lunch." A couple of weeks later she arrived at SeaTac Airport and spent a week with my family and me.

As we were sharing stories that day in San Francisco, at one point Inge looked at me, laughed and said, "Do you realize we are talking like old friends?" How does that happen? Sometimes we have friends for years and that friendship stays at a superficial level. Then there are those chance meetings where your spirits connect before you even get to really know each other. It happened that day with Inge and me.

The following year Inge and I shared a booth at the Trade Center. On Saturday afternoon she had a wedding to attend with her husband. After breakfast she drove me to the BART station. As always the station was crowded with people. She gave me directions how to get on the train and we said our goodbyes at the door. I crossed the crowded, noisy room and stepped onto the escalator. As it slowly began carrying me up to the next level I heard someone shouting my name. And I knew it was my friend Inge. I turned around to see her jumping up and down waving at me with this huge smile on her face and shouting, "Have a great day. I love you." At that moment my heart bonded to hers. Inge's life if filled with richness and she shares that richness with her friends. As I settled into my seat on BART I couldn't control the smile on my face. My mind traveled back to the previous year when Inge showed up at my booth at the Trade Center and thought, "What if I hadn't showed up on the last day?" Just think what I would have missed. This beautiful friendship!

Inge came from Germany in her early twenties and was a pattern designer for Simplicity in New York City for several years. When she met her husband they moved to Walnut Creek, just outside of San Francisco. Today she is an artist and travels all over the world taking her paints with her and capturing on canvas the highlights of her trips.

She also is the mother of two beautiful children.

What do I love about my friend? Inge lives life with gusto and Inge is real. She has this beautiful energy that carries her through life. She is positive and has a truly happy spirit. Inge has a contagious laugh, and her eyes dance when she speaks. Laughter comes easily to her. She has her own style. Inge is classy. Inge lives life with a passion and lives her dream.

CAITLIN

It was 8 a.m. on a Monday morning and there was a light tapping on my front door. I opened the door to find my young friend Caitlin standing there. Caitlin is my neighbor and one of my best friends. She is nine years old. She smiled and looked at me and said, "This summer I'm going to study acting and then I'm going to be an actor!" Caitlin is an artist and writer and a great storyteller. Her stories are filled with animation. So, yes, I could certainly see her studying acting and one day becoming an actor. During our conversations she will stop and ask "did you ever think about?" and then she'll go off and build a story about something we just talked about. She has a special talent for creating. Her mind is always working. Caitlin plays the piano and is on the swim team.

Caitlin is my errand buddy. One of our favorite things to do is eat ice cream at Baskin and Robbins. We also play chess together. We hang out at McDonalds eating cheeseburgers and drinking chocolate milk shakes. Sometimes we stop at the lake and go wading in the water. Hanging out with Caitlin is one of my favorite things to do because it's easy. And she's so real! Kids see life in such a fresh way and they speak what's on their mind without editing. They stretch our hearts and fill up our souls. Their feelings are always visible. They laugh so easy and aren't afraid to cry. They are filled with trust and loyalty and forgiveness.

When Caitlin brings her sister Isabel over to visit they like to play hide and seek with my husband Phil and I. Our house is filled with bodies running here and there and squeezing into places they never should fit into. Giggles fill the air.

What have I learned from my friend? Life is filled with opportunities and NOTHING is impossible if you dare to dream.

Caitlin, this poem is for you.

Help me to be
What I want to be,
Help me achieve
The dreams that I've dreamed.
Help me to reach
As high as I can,
To reach my potential
As only I can.
Help me climb mountains
That seem too high
And push me onward
To reach for the sky.
Help me to stretch
Beyond what I see,
Help me to be-
Me.

MARY

Several years ago I received a phone call from a friend asking if I would interview a friend of hers. She felt her friend had an amazing story to tell. One week later I found myself sitting in the home of the 75-year-old "star" of the McDonald's "The New Kid" commercials. With a history of back surgery, cancer and a 40-year marriage that ended in divorce, Mary has shown that you can do anything you want to do, if you want it badly enough. Somewhere in the midst of the interview that afternoon Mary and I became friends.

At age 73 Mary headed for L.A. in her van to fulfill her dream of becoming a professional actress. Her destination was the American Academy of Art. Uncertain of where she wanted to study she headed for San Francisco and interviewed at the Academy of Art. Finally deciding she wanted to study in the Seattle area where her home is, she applied at Cornish College of the Arts. She graduated with a Professional Acting and Bachelor of Fine Arts Degree in Theatre. After graduating from Cornish Mary wrote and starred in "No Ties to Bind" which she performed throughout the state of Washington and in local prisons.

From there she went on to do local radio commercials, several Hallmark, Hospital, Bartell, and Sonics TV commercials and performed a variety of roles in live theatre. And today at the age of 88 she models for fashion magazines.

Mary is a graduate of Political Science Pre-law, and holds a Master's Degree in Social Work. She has proven there are no limits except those that are self-imposed.

Mary works out at the gym three times a week.

While attending a play Mary was in, my husband leaned over to me and said, "Mary has great legs, doesn't she?" I turned to him and said, "and so what do you think of the play?"

A few years ago our friend stopped by to see Mary in the middle of the afternoon and found her up on her roof just "checking things out."

Mary has attended our annual Christmas party for the past 11 years. Our friends wait for Mary's arrival to hear about her latest adventure. When Mary arrives anywhere, she doesn't just show up like most of us do. She enters a room with grace and poise and everyone stops to notice.

Age has no meaning to Mary. And she doesn't put limits on what she can do. She just does *everything*!

What have I learned from my friend? Age doesn't define you. Only if you let it. If you live life without reservation, you just keep doing what you've always done. You get what you expect from life. Mary expects adventure, and she finds it. She expects full days, interesting days. She creates them. Mary doesn't think about dying.

She thinks about living.

One evening my husband and I were having dinner with Mary at her home and we were admiring the tile floor in her dining room. This is a "BIG" room. She started to laugh and told us how after having breast cancer she came home from the hospital and immediately began laying the tile floor, crawling around on her hands and knees. I asked her, "Weren't you tired and really sore?" Meaning from the surgery.

She replied, "You know, by the time I finished the floor my arm was a little sore." That was 30 years ago!

What do I love about my friend? She doesn't run from life. She confronts it and embraces it. And keeps on doing what she's always done. Living life fully.

When I asked Mary, "Where does your passion for life come from?" she answered, "Her parents and the way she was raised, her 3 children, 7 grandchildren, and 10 great-grandchildren."

Mary closed our interview that afternoon with the following words, "The quality of your life is in proportion to the quality of commitment you make to it".

Mary has an amazing spirit!

CHOOSING TO BE REAL

When you are content to be simply yourself and don't compare or compete, everybody will respect.

Lao-Tzu

This I so believe. When we truly move into ourselves, accepting and liking who we are, letting go of the competition and always trying to be the "something" so we can be accepted, we move through life with ease, and people who show up in our lives are so different than the ones we attracted before.

The phrase "real women" is popping up everywhere today, in magazines, on TV commercials and in women's conversations. It's in the air like a fall virus. As a Life Coach, I encounter women from all walks of life and their stories are all the same. They want to surround themselves with women who are positive and real. I began noticing in conversations with friends and clients that they were all saying the same thing. Even my male clients. They want to spend time with people that lift them up and are genuine.

Does it mean that we just start dropping friends carelessly? No.

But it does mean that we can give ourselves permission to remove ourselves from these toxic friendships. I call these friends "crazy makers". They exhaust us and steal our energy. When they leave our home or we hang up our phone from a conversation with them, we feel drained or even depressed. When we keep these "crazy makers" in our life, we begin living a life that is not our own. When we feel the need to meet the expectations of these people we undervalue ourselves and misplace our own values. Sometimes friendship becomes more of an obligation than a pleasure. When friendship is healthy we experience it with grace and ease. I have found, as I have grown and changed, sometimes my friendships have changed.

When we become real, we show the humanness we all possess, if we let our guard down and dare to be real.

I DWELL IN POSSIBILITY

I have learned that we often succeed because of our friends. They become our cheerleaders.

The idea for this book was born one rainy night as I sat by the fire reading. I wrote the first chapter that night and believed with everything in my heart that the rest of the chapters would follow, if I would just show up at my computer every morning. I felt a commitment like I had never felt before. As I finished that first chapter I said a silent payer, "Father you are my source, I am your instrument."

The next morning a friend called and I shared with her about my writing and my dream for this book. She asked me to send it to her that day. That was on Friday. It arrived in her mailbox the following day. I came home late Saturday afternoon. My husband said, "There's a message on the answering machine. I think you should listen to it". I walked over to it and hit the play button. It was the voice of my friend Carla. Her message began — "I went out to the mail box this afternoon and found the first

SANDRA J. GOOSELAW

chapter of your book. I'm sitting by the fire reading it with tears streaming down my face. I can't wait to get the next chapter." Every week for the next several months I mailed off the next chapter to her. What kept me writing was her belief and constant encouragement in me. And she held me accountable to this project. Every week I'd receive my writing back with comments and affirmations written all over it. Carla had been a client of mine four years ago and we became fast friends. I believe our life is a journey and each part of it is in preparation for something further down the road. I also believe she was placed in my life four years ago to become my cheerleader for this project. I know with all my heart it would not have happened without her. I love the song, "It takes a Village." It's so true! There's very little we do on our own. We think we do, but if we look at our life closely, we will find there's always something or someone greater than us in the background, cheering us on.

I am so grateful for all my friends and family that believe in me when I don't. Who don't take "no" for an answer when I feel discouraged. They see open doors when I sometimes see them closed. They are the village that makes up my life and I am eternally thankful for each one of them. Each one of us has our own village surrounding us. Sometimes we just can't see it.

48

THE BEST PART OF LIFE IS USUALLY FOUND IN THE DETAILS

It's in the details of life that our memories are built

I was raised with four brothers so I was conditioned from the beginning to live with adventure and to be just a little bit braver. Something deep inside me has always wanted the best that life can offer. Not in material things, but in the quality of life. And I can't remember a day when that desire wasn't there.

I have been a writer most of my life and as a writer I always carry a pad and pencil with me wherever I go. This simple habit reminds me to notice the details around me. I have found that, *"the best of life"* is usually found in the details.

The following stories are some of the details from my life.

Some of my friends have cleaning ladies. I have entertained the thought and have even gone so far as to interview one. But when it came right down to hiring one, something inside of me just couldn't do it. What I have realized is it's the every day, ordinary chores that keep me centered. I love the smell of fresh laundry (you know, when you take it out of the dryer and it's still warm and you bury your face in it) Yup! I do that! And the smell of fresh bread baking. When I need to relieve stress I find myself in the kitchen baking bread. I realize to many women that is a strange phenomenon, but it works for me. There's something about the kneading that quiets my spirit. I know, I could have a bread maker, but it's the touching of the fresh dough and the kneading that is soothing to me. And there's something about the smell of yeast. I love being a participator in the details of my home and of our family life. It's different for all of us. The key is to find what works for you.

We had a nanny the first nine years of my life. Her name was Clara. My mom was a professional. The luxury of having Clara was that when my mom was home she gave us 100% of her time. Clara was short and plump and filled our home with the smells of fresh baked bread and chocolate chip cookies. My mother also loved to bake. I'm pretty sure that's where my love for baking came from.

Every week there were freshly washed clothes hanging on the clothesline in our back yard. Today that would be a rare commodity. There's something in homemade baked goods and doing the laundry that feels solid to me. Maybe it's because it reminds me of growing up in a large family surrounded by the ordinary things in life.

I have a friend who, whenever she passes by my house stops, knocks on my front door and when I open it, says, "Don't have time to stay, but just wanted to give you a hug." That makes my day. One of the details.

Our youngest daughter lives in this high-powered business world. At the dinner table I listen to her use power words like "thinking out of the box", "on board", "24-7", and my heart searches for the little girl I remember that has been replaced by the sophistication of her new world. But as the busyness of the day transitions into family time and we all gather in the den with our quilts and pillows to watch movies together, I watch her demeanor soften. Soon I realize she's missing and I wander down stairs to find her curled up on the couch in the living room. She invites me over and I curl up beside her. As my nose brushes her forehead I recognize the familiar smell from the days when I would hold her and snuggle and we would read stories together. One of my *favorite* details.

I came home one day from buying office supplies and set the bag in my office closet. A week later I went to get something out of it and a note fell out. The clerk who had waited on me had tucked this handwritten note in my bag along with the things I had purchased. It read as follows:

Fahtima's thought for the day :)

I am only one, but still I am one. I cannot do everything, but still I can do something. And because I cannot do everything, I will not refuse to do the something I can do.:) Keep trying for what you really want!

I had just opened my new business and this was just the encouragement I needed to hear. This was ten years ago and the note is still taped on the cabinet door next to my computer. It is a constant reminder to me to always keep trying for what I really want in life. It also reminded me of the impact that words have on us and how a stranger had filled my heart with encouragement by taking the time to write this little note and send it home with me. And her timing was perfect. What I learned that day—I wanted to take the encouragement she gave to me and pass it on to others with my own words, because we don't know when someone else may need our encouragement, and just maybe, our timing would be perfect.

When my husband goes on a business trip, the week before he leaves, he starts dropping cards in the mail so while he's away I receive a card in the mail every day. That helps me to feel his presence even though he's away. He's a romantic.

In the spring I wait for the appearance of the first leaves on the birch tree outside my office window, and the first sign of flowers as they push their way up through the dirt in the flower bed below. The squirrels that are busy in the yard collecting twigs and racing up the big evergreens to build nests preparing for the spring litter of baby squirrels, and then later show up at our back door to collect their supply of peanuts for the day. When I step outside on a rainy day, I stop to smell the fresh air that comes with the rain. I love stormy days when I can hear the sound of the wind howling through the evergreens in my front yard. I love the coziness of winter. I think I was born a nester. I love spring and preparing the yard for summer. And then I begin looking forward to fall when the yard will take care of itself and I can curl up by a crackling fire and read my favorite book. I love the details of nature.

Special moments with each of my children and my husband. **My favorite details.**

I REALLY WISH I COULD, BUT I DON'T WANT TO

(This came from a conversation with a friend one day)

The Art of saying no

I can remember in my early thirties, as a wife and young mother with three small children, being on every committee there was to be on, and teaching Sunday School. Always saying "yes" when I was asked to do something. Not wanting to let anyone down. Thinking that was just what you were supposed to do. When what I really wanted to do was say "no." Often feeling overwhelmed with all the commitments, but doing it anyway. Then one day I was reading an article that talked about over-commitment and the art of saying "no". Boy, did my ears perk up! What a gift that article gave me that day. I began practicing the art of saying "no."

Since that day I have learned to pick and choose what I commit to, and then really enjoy what I'm involved in.

How many times have we said "yes" when a friend calls, when what we really wanted to say was "no." Because we didn't want to hurt her feelings. The truth is, if they are a good friend, they understand when we say, "Thank you for thinking of me, but I would rather stay home today". Some days we just need that time to "hang out with ourselves" and be alone. I know I do. I love those special days that I choose to unplug the phone, read by the fire or put in one of my favorite movies and remove myself from the outside world. It is so refreshing and fills me up to face life again. Ultimately we are each responsible for our own health and well-being and its up to us to nurture and take care of ourselves.

Like the cliché "Reinventing the Wheel", there are times I feel the need to reinvent my life. As women it is so easy to over extend ourselves and soon we are on overload. I work out of a home-based office and it's easy to say yes to every client who calls for an appointment. When I find myself feeling stretched and over-tired, mentally looking for a place to go into hibernation, I know something is out of balance in my life. It's a skill to keep our professional life, family life, health (exercise, eating right, rest), and social life all in balance. When I find myself in this place I sit down with my journal and begin making a new plan for my life. Busy schedules and projects often dictate this necessity. I give myself permission to fine-tune my schedule, keeping only those things that are really important to me. There are always the necessities, which are a part of life, but I find there are a lot of activities that would make life easier if they weren't there. I try to remember to honor myself enough to self-protect from the stresses that creep in unnoticed until one day life becomes exhausting instead of fun.

Some days "you just gotta wear pajamas all day, sip hot chocolate and be a guilt-free napper."

SPEND AS LITTLE TIME AS POSSIBLE ON THINGS THAT JUST DON'T MATTER

As I sit here writing, dust is collecting on my furniture and as I wander through the house, I wonder, "Was that a cobweb I saw hanging in the corner of my living room?" In her book, "Gifts From The Sea" Anne Morrow Lindbergh talks about where we place our values and how we spend our time. Her motto is simplify, simplify, simplify. She has a beach home where she goes to relax and write. The floors are wood and often covered with sand. Her artwork being done by the local spiders that weave designs across her walls in careless splendor. She talks about how we gather art for our homes that we have to insure and install home alarm systems so no one steals our expensive purchases while we are away on vacation. We live in big homes that are filled with expensive furniture that takes hours to maintain. She challenges her readers to simplify their lives and ask themselves, "What's really important in life?"

I have always been impressed with my friends who choose the simpler path. They seem to put off the chores that I get so lost in, to nurture their friendships or hobbies, or just dare to do whatever. I've heard it said a little untidiness manifests itself in comfort, while perfection manifests itself in migraines. I believe this is so true. People are more comfortable in homes that are just a little bit out of order, and feel lived in. I can remember early on in my marriage "walking around puffy rugs in our living room so I wouldn't leave footprints on them". I know this sounds a little weird, that's why I'm mentioning it, so that *you know* that *I know* that it sounds weird. I look back on that today and wonder, "What do you suppose I was thinking?" I have sooo relaxed since that time in my life.

I like to live with flexibility and spontaneity. If

I have to decide between chores and time with my children, husband or friends, chores are rarely an option.

FRIENDS

Angels sent to watch over us

What fills my life with energy and enthusiasm? Having friends of all ages. My youngest friend is eleven and my oldest friend is 90. And in between are women of all ages and from all walks of life. All different sizes and shapes and a mixture of personalities. And somehow I am blessed to be in the middle of all these awesome and beautiful women and to call them "friend." Each one brings her own unique flavor and richness to my life.

Early on in my life I made a conscious effort to surround myself with positive friends. They lift me up and help me to reach my highest potential. They give me energy when mine is gone. Our friends mirror back to us who we are, so we can become *all* of who we are meant to be.

I have heard it said many times, "If we have one true friend, we are truly rich and blessed."

What do I look for in a friend?

Number one...someone who is real! They let you see their imperfections. Being around these friends is so easy because they help us to accept our own imperfections and they let us see theirs.

Someone who:

Lives life with a huge sense of passion!

Lives life with grace.

Is spiritual.

Is honest and trustworthy.

Shares tears.

One who doesn't just settle for what life gives them, but dares to be all that they can be. Most of us live in the box. They dare to step out of the box. They dare to speak out when the rest of us would be quiet and polite.

Who takes life lightly and laughs a lot!

Loves chocolate as much as I do!

Who dares to "dance"!

I have a friend, whenever I have conversations with her, I know she's listening 100%. She asks for the details. She wants to know more. She reads between the lines. When I ask for advice I trust what she gives me. She sees life in a practical, real way and answers with honesty. She says what she believes will help me and not what she thinks I want to hear.

I have another friend that just says it like it is and is so real. I appreciate her candor and honesty. She has a tender, sensitive spirit and speaks from her heart.

My friend Betty is my counselor. She helps me to see things clearly when my perspective is clouded. She takes the emotion out of the situation and helps me see the facts in a real way.

My friend Jill gives me permission to curl up by a fire on a rainy day and read all day. She tells me I don't have to be responsible for anything that day and I don't have to answer my phone. I can stay in pajamas all day. She is a guilt free napper and teaching me to be one too. I love the easy way she moves though life and enjoys the details. A part of her moves in slow motion savoring the things that most of us miss or are too busy to take time for. She invites me to partner with her in these life-savoring experiences. She sips hot chocolate in the midst of winter rainstorms. It's the uncluttered moments that hold life's richest treasures, if we just stop to notice.

Two years ago one of my daughters and I were flying to San Diego to meet the Minnesota girls for our Girls' weekend. After our plane landed we headed to baggage claim to collect our suitcases and then walked out to the sidewalk where our airporter was waiting for us. We took our seats and the driver climbed in behind the wheel. As he started the engine a woman and her husband began tapping on the door. The driver opened the door and asked if they had a ticket. She said they didn't and the driver informed her they would have to wait for the next van. She was persistent and he stepped out to speak to her. After several minutes I found him opening the side door and letting her in to sit down beside me. We were anxious to get to our hotel. As the van began pulling away from the curb she turned to me, introduced herself and apologized for detaining all of us. Then the most amazing conversation began between us. We were two strangers sitting on a van and we began sharing life's most intimate thoughts. She was in her late twenties, with long blonde hair and an athletic body. She was pretty and outgoing and looked like she was living the perfect life. Here is the story she shared with me on that 30-minute ride from the airport to our hotel. She had a pregnancy out of wedlock in high school and had an abortion and now was happily married with two beautiful daughters. Her dream was to share her story with high school girls and be a mentor to girls who found themselves in the same situation. Hoping to help them make a different choice. She had never been athletic and after her second baby was born she decided her body needed some attention and she began walking. Walking led to running. She never dreamed she would be a runner. She began running marathons and winning and found she was a natural runner. The following month she was running a marathon in Hawaii. She looked at me and said, "Isn't it amazing where life takes us?" As our van pulled into the parking lot at our hotel we hugged each other and said our goodbyes. As I stepped off the van she said, "I'm not ready for this conversation to end yet." I felt the same way. I began walking away and pulling my suitcase behind me when I heard a man shouting, "Ma'am." I turned around to find the bus driver running after me. He said the lady on the bus wanted to talk to me. I walked back to the van and she asked for my phone number and said, "Let's keep in touch." I went home anticipating that phone call. It never came. Our meeting that day was "serendipity." Will we meet again someday? I don't know. That 30-minute ride was the highlight of my trip because my heart connected with a stranger's heart and in that moment we became friends and shared deep experiences with each other. Something in each of us trusted the other. I believe as we go through life people are placed in unsuspecting places and they minister to us and maybe we in turn minister to them.

These are extraordinary moments and cause us to say, "Life is exceptional!" If we are sensitive to these times, soon our life is filled with these "chance encounters."

What did I learn from this new friend? She dared to be

real. She spoke from her heart and trusted I wouldn't judge her. She learned from this challenge in her life and became stronger because of it. And now she wants to share it with the world.

I have learned that we all have different experiences in life. Some choose to keep that experience inside them. And then there are "those" that choose to go the extra mile. They choose to be brave enough to share their story, hoping to make a difference in someone else's life, and not worry that they may be judged by the world. Because the truth is, there's always someone around that feels the need to judge others. But these few that "dare to make a difference", tell their story anyway.

What if the driver had chosen not to let this couple on the airporter that afternoon in San Diego? I would have missed this "chance encounter." Sometimes these encounters are only for that moment in time. But they leave footprints on our hearts forever.

IF YOU DON'T HAVE A SISTER— FIND ONE AND ADOPT HER

For some of us, sisters are born into our family. A sister bond is like no other bond we share with another human being. As women we all need a place where we can go and empty our heart and soul unedited and know that is a safe place? We don't need to set boundaries of "please don't share this with anyone", because we know she won't. Relationships like this are rare. If we are lucky we find this place in a special sister. Some of these sisters come in the form of biological sisters, and sometimes they come as friends whom we have adopted as sisters. I didn't purposefully go on the hunt for a sister. She just showed up one day and we adopted each other! And I'm so thankful for this special "sisterhood" we share. We met through two of our children. It began with short phone calls delivering messages between our kids. Then one night we met for dinner, and the rest is history. That was 12 years ago. I have found that the best friendships just happen. They don't take any work and from the beginning you feel that bond of trust and sisterhood. I don't believe they evolve over night, but usually from the beginning you sense something special there. That's how it was when I met my friend Betty. Our hearts connected from the beginning. And there was this effortless comfort in her presence. She is the kind of friend you love to hang with, shop with, and sip wine with, sitting in front of a crackling fire, sharing stories. Sisters can sense what you mean with your heart when your mouth is saying something different. They listen, edit, and translate it into what you really meant to say, and toss the rest away. You dare to speak the truth of your feelings. I don't think biological sisters always end up being the kind of sister I'm talking about. Being family does not mean we always connect in this way or feel the freedom to say just anything with each other. I love the women in my life who share the realities of their lives. I don't know that they do it easily, but they do it. Somehow their sharing comes directly from their heart and they dare to do it, because that is who they are. When we speak candidly it sets us up to be vulnerable, but what a gift we give to those other women in our lives, because we give them permission to open up, and we become a safe place for them. We appear real. I am always in awe of these women when I'm a part of their honest conversations.

Betty is one of those friends. She is sensitive and highly intuitive. She sees my tears when there are none to be seen. She sees laughter in my eyes when no chuckle is audible and hears music in a silent room. Her spirit is happy and there's always an abundance of laughter when we're together. We laugh at life, but more often at each other. Betty has the ability to see life with a really clear vision, and helps me to keep my vision clear. We often find ourselves in each other's guest rooms for an overnighter. Our husbands go off to bed leaving us curled up on the couch knowing we'll be there until the wee hours of the morning chatting. Our friendship is easy.

We share the same blonde hair, the same blue eyes, and even the same middle name. I didn't purposely go on the hunt for a sister. She just showed up one day, and we adopted each other.

FAITH

Faith and God are very personal and different for each one of us. For me, faith is about believing in something bigger than myself, and knowing that I am not on this journey alone. That there is grace waiting for me when I stumble and fall. That there's forgiveness when I could have made a better choice. That God is always there when it feels like nobody else is.

There's never a day goes by that I don't talk to God. More than talking, I experience God in most all my waking moments. It's a feeling that goes beyond anything else that I have ever known in life.

We all find and experience God in our own way, but for each of us it's connecting with a higher power.

Throughout my life I have always chosen to follow my own instincts. The ones I believe God places in us the day we are born, to help guide us through life and make decisions that are best for us. When my still, small voice speaks, I'm glad I have the courage to listen. I know life always works out the way it was meant to be.

I deeply value spirituality. Spirituality is our reaching out to God and finding a relationship there. And a knowing that He is always there reaching out to us. He is always accessible. We just need to reach back.

I find inner peace in my faith and a knowing that God has a perfect plan for my life.

For me, it's not about religion; it's about a relationship with my creator. Faith is about surrender, love, forgiveness and grace.

I know that God can dream a bigger dream for me than I could ever dream for myself. For me it's about walking in faith, knowing there is someone bigger than myself walking beside me, whose heart is to help me succeed at the dream he placed in my heart the day I was born.

I wouldn't change my life. I don't believe in accidents or things that could have been different. I believe they are all part of my individual journey. I've made mistakes. But all of it makes me who I am today. I can't change even a small part and remain who I am.

Grace—unearned love that goes before us, that greets us on our way. Grace meets us where we are, but doesn't leave us where it found us.

I try to share the grace God gives to me with all those who cross my path. To replace judgment with understanding, gossip with praise. I don't always succeed, but I try harder the next time.

IT'S OK TO WALK ALONE

Let the world know you as you are, not as you think you should be, because sooner or later, if you are posing, you will forget the pose, and then where are you?

Fanny Brice

There's so much freedom in "Walking Your Own Walk." Most of us grow up believing we need to follow the crowd and fit in. Wear the right clothes, be seen at the right places, have the right friends. Fit the perfect mold. I learned a long time ago it takes a lot of energy to try to be perfect. The truth is, no matter how hard we try, there is no way to be perfect. And how exhausting it is to follow the crowd. In the end I knew that I wanted to live my life being "real." The process takes a lot of deep housecleaning inside ourselves and confronting old beliefs. But the result is life changing. As I evolved into a more real person I noticed the friends I attracted were different, richer, and real. I

found a new inner peace and confidence. In the midst of all that changing I found me. ***What a gift!***
"Follow your own path, and let people talk" Dante

MOTHERHOOD—The Journey of a Lifetime

What I know for sure. The two things in life that we all hope to succeed at and yet are given no training for are marriage and parenting. All of our decisions are made by trial and error. It's a wonder we all survive. When I became a mom, I believed that God had put those natural mom instincts in me the day I was born, to make the right decisions, if I just listened carefully to my heart. When my children were little, that worked pretty well. But I found, the older they became, the decisions were harder and the consequences more severe, if I made the wrong choice. What I've learned along the way. That listening is often better than words. That our children's interpretation of our words is *often* very different than our intention when we say them. To really listen when they speak, and truly hear what they're saying. To honor their unique and individual personalities. That I am here to guide them, but not to make all their decisions. To try to let them do it their way. Knowing that's how they learn and that they will become stronger because of their mistakes.

Especially when they leave home for the first time, to give them the grace and space to find their way in the world, find out who they are and what they want to become. To give them the same free will to make their own choices that God gives to me every day. To be there as their cheerleader when they stumble and fall and make mistakes. To never place judgment, but be their encourager. I am proud of each of my children for daring to try the world on in different ways, not be afraid of challenge and daring to do it their way.

Most of us as women have the potential of giving birth to a baby. But I believe being a mom is born *"in the heart."* Whether our children come to us as biological babies or are a gift from an unknown woman who had the courage to give up her baby for so many different reasons.

Our first baby girl arrived at SeaTac airport at 9am. on a sunny, spring Friday morning. She was a beautiful baby, all cheeks and full of boundless joy. She had jet-black hair and these big brown eyes. And she was mine. We received a phone call two days earlier saying she was arriving. I felt myself going into labor the moment I placed the phone back on the rack. It was a different kind of labor than most women go through. I was so excited for this little human being to arrive, yet fearful of all the unknowns of being a mom.

It was an overwhelming feeling when I became a mom for the first time. The idea seemed so good, but I quickly found out the dream was so much different than the reality. At least for a while. But I soon realized, "love" transcends all fears and feelings. As young women our visual picture of being a mom is usually only focused on the snuggling and holding our baby, how good they smell, thinking they will always smile and coo and sleep. Then reality sets in and they keep us up all night, and spit up all over us. Sometimes no matter what we do, we're unable to calm them. They teach us patience and fill our hearts with a kind of love that no other human being can place there. I always felt that it was such a privilege to be a mom. Not a *right* that I had as a woman. But a privilege God gave me.

I remember receiving the picture of our first daughter, and falling in love with the little girl in that picture. I carried her picture everywhere with me and showed it to anyone who would stop long enough for me to get it out. After a while, I'm sure my friends wanted to run the other way when they saw me coming, thinking, "Oh no! Here she comes with that picture again! Run! Run!" The thing is, that never changed. With each new picture of the next child we were adopting, their picture traveled with me in my purse and I'm sure my friends still felt the same way when they saw me coming. Here she comes *again* with another picture. The amazing thing I realized as a mom, is when each child arrived God filled my heart to overflowing with more love to share with that new little person. There was always enough love for everyone. Some days I thought my heart would burst. It's amazing how He evens out all that love between however many children we are blessed to have and we love them all equally.

When Kym arrived my nights were her days. So she wanted to be awake when I wanted to sleep. And she wanted to sleep when I wanted her to be awake. She arrived with a virus and cried a lot. Soon I had her virus, *and* I wanted to cry a lot. It was hard to figure out how to do all the things I was used to doing with this little baby on my hip most of the day. My emotions were like a roller coaster ride. One minute I loved being a mom and the next minute I felt challenged. But one thing I've realized in life is that any time we make a change or add something new in our life there is always an adjustment period. Another thing I've learned is when we stretch ourselves to do something uncomfortable or different, our character becomes stronger and our life becomes richer. When we dare to step out of our comfort zone something inside of us changes and we are never the same.

About a month after her arrival I was still struggling with these feelings of being a new mom. One afternoon we were visiting my mother. As she was playing on the floor with Kym she scooped her up and hugged her tight and said, "I love you." As she did that something stirred inside my heart and I knew my bonding with my new daughter had begun.

With each new child I realized I experienced the same feelings of uneasiness. One day I was sharing this with a friend. And she told me what I was feeling was normal. She said, "Think about the mobile that we hang over our children's cribs. When you buy them they are evenly balanced. If you add an extra piece they are thrown off balance. It's the same when you add another member to the family. Before they arrive the family is in balance. When you add that new child the family is thrown off balance for awhile, until every one gets adjusted to each other." That made sense to me.

We adopted two more children from Korea. I found as

each child arrived with his or her personality already formed, it took lots of giving and taking. Lots of accepting and learning and growing together. But I also realized that is what being a family is all about. When our son Min arrived he was four years old. I wanted to hold and snuggle him the same way I did our baby daughter when she arrived. As I would hold him and rock him I knew he was waiting for the moment when he could escape my clutches and be set free. I learned each child is different and they touch our heart in their own way. They teach us what they need from us. And it's not always the same.

I knew from the beginning of motherhood my heart had room for three. I think we all have a number in there somewhere that doesn't go away until our heart is satisfied.

Four years after Min arrived, my heart started nudging me again and I found myself filling out all those pages for the adoption application. I was hoping this time I could just somehow skip that part of the process. Maybe that's like morning sickness for us adoption moms. I think as adopting moms we go through all the same feelings of pregnancy. They just come in a different form. When I received each picture the excitement I felt must compare to what a pregnant mom experiences when she's told she is pregnant. Each time I stood at the airport window and saw their plane touching down, I believed it must compare to being in the labor room and hearing the doctor shout, "she's entering the birth canal." It's this process that helps prepare us for motherhood. By the time they arrive we are so excited and our unconditional love is firmly in place.

This time we decided to adopt a child from New York. But I believe with all my heart the day I was born God already had these three babies planned for my life, and in His mysterious way He would get us all together, even from across the ocean. With our last child He decided I needed to experience a premature baby because Tahnya arrived in three months. The sad part was I didn't have all those months to chase my friends around with her picture like I did with my first two. I'm sure *they* were disappointed!! This beautiful little four-year-old Korean girl arrived so full of spunk and spirit. And that's what I still love so much about her today. She has always lived life with such passion. She dares to share her emotions. She is so real. She has taught me so much about life. To be in the moment and don't worry how the world perceives you. She has this gift of embracing the moment.

Then when I thought my family was complete a stepson came into my life. Its funny how we start down this road of life with our plans all in place and somewhere along the way the road takes a curve and we find ourselves in a new place. Around that curve I found Jason. After Tahnya arrived I sometimes felt a longing for one more child, but never pursued those feelings. My heart was prepared for his arrival. I just didn't know it. He came in the form of a 19 year old. And found a place in my heart so easily.

What I wanted to teach my children most was to notice the details in life. Don't be a bystander. Be a participator. And above all "be happy!" I wanted them to notice the smell of rain in the air when they stepped out the front door on the first fall morning. I wanted to tell them don't wait for the big events in life to make you happy, but live in the details. Make every day exceptional. I wanted their journey to be filled with peace, with wonder, with curiosity, and most of all satisfaction. I wanted them to be truly happy with life and what it gave them. I wanted them to know you have to go after what you want in life. It doesn't come and find you. And don't just settle. I wanted them to know that the day they were born God placed a dream in their heart. And He wanted them to realize and live that dream one day. I think many of us *dream* of living our dream. I didn't want my kids to miss *living* their dream.

I wanted to protect them from pain and having to learn from life's lessons. But life is like a muscle. If you don't work you're muscles they become weak. I wanted them to know, it's the same with life. It's the challenges that make us strong. And I wanted them to be strong. To look at life's challenges as opportunities. To be better because of them and not diminished by them.

I wanted them all to have the perfect mate that would cherish them for who they are and love them unconditionally.

I wanted them to have the best that life could give them.

Webster's definition of a mother is:
A female parent; something that gives origin or rise to something else.

As I think about the second part of the definition I realize it is saying that we as women have the physical ability to create life and then with that life, we're given this awesome responsibility, but also this very special *privilege* of sharing in this intimate relationship of nurturing and creating a healthy human being. What a gift!

What have I realized? Being a mom is the best thing that ever happened to me. And I would not have missed this ride for anything.

As I have taught my children, they in turn have taught me so much about life, and love, giving and forgiving,

When our children left home, we gave them wings and our position changed in their lives. We gave them to God knowing He had a perfect plan for each one and that he would always be there to catch them when they fall. Then we moved to the sidelines. The hardest position to hold. What I've learned is that it's the hard times that take us to the really good places.

Always let your children know how much they are loved. Tell them every day. And let them know that you consider them to be your greatest gifts.

HOME—Our Retreat from the World

When I close the front door behind me, I leave the busy world outside and step into my sanctuary. The sound of the fountain greets me as my eyes take in the soft colors of creams and taupes that fill our home. The peaceful atmosphere nurtures my soul.

Our home is a place where my family finds retreat from their busy lives. A place where they can refresh their spirits. A space filled with peace and beauty.

One of the favorite places in our home to all of us is our library. We are all avid readers and love to curl up with a good book next to the crackling fire with a mug of hot chocolate.

Most all of my life I have worked at creating beauty in the spaces I have lived in and filled them with peace and tranquility. I can remember when I was 11 years old going out to my dad's shed and rummaging around until I found his left over cans of paint. I searched until I found a color that intrigued me. And then I would head to my bedroom and paint it a new color. During my growing up years my bedroom walls were my canvas where I experimented with color and design. At a young age I realized my surroundings contributed to my sense of well-being and contentment.

I am a visual person and easily respond to my surroundings. I like getting up early in the morning when the rest of the world is still asleep. I begin every morning by taking a stroll through my home, soaking up the ambiance that nurtures my spirit. I often stop to sit in my living room for a few minutes where palm trees hang lazily over my couches and my eyes take in the garden just outside my window where squirrels are busy scampering up the trees, with their mouths filled with treasures gathered from the yard. My next stop is my office where I do my morning journaling. Morning pages are a place where I connect with myself before the busyness of my day begins.

Our surroundings have a big impact on our feelings of well-being and contribute to our good health. When our home is orderly and peaceful, our spirit and body respond to that atmosphere. There are four things we should have in our home. Good books, good music, fine art and fresh flowers. When our bodies and minds are relaxed and nurtured, our bodies respond by being healthy.

MORNING PAGES/JOURNALING

I started journaling about 25 years ago and my journal has become my best friend, my constant companion. What I have learned over the years is the power in words and how writing dreams and goals down makes them happen. One of my favorite books is "Write It Down, Make It Happen" by Henriette Anne Klauser. She teaches the art of writing things down by creating an initial plan and then writing into resolution where you begin to see results.

There is no right or wrong way to journal. It's just a place to get your thoughts and feelings out of you and onto paper. Somewhere in the midst of that process I find solutions, relieve stress, capture a moment, or make a plan. Sometimes I do something Julia Cameron in her book "The Artist's Way" calls "brain drain." Just writing and rambling to clear my brain. She recommends a form of writing called "Morning Pages" that she does every morning as soon as she gets out of bed. It's a place where first thing in the morning she clears her head by writing down all the thoughts or feelings that get in the way and clutter our brains and prevent us from accomplishing the things we want to accomplish.

For me personally, journaling is an honoring of who I am by taking time to focus on my life, my feelings, what's important to me, setting goals and staying focused. Seeing all of those areas as important and separating myself from all the roles in my life as friend, wife, and mother and honoring the person God created me to be.

What I find in writing is that when I detail my desires or goals on paper I put a plan in motion. I believe whatever we give our attention to, we succeed at. When I leave them in my head they just seem to circle without any form. I have learned there is so much power in words, and in paying attention to the things we want in life. Believing they can happen if we give attention to them. By journaling I keep my focus on where I want to go and what's important to me.

TRADITIONS

I love family traditions, traditions with friends, building a history of memorable events or relationships with those closest to me. And creating new traditions and friendships.

Nine years ago I lost a brother to cancer. After his death my oldest daughter came to me and said, "Mom, we need to stay close as a family." What she was saying was we need to stay connected. When we lose the matriarchs and patriarchs of our families the baton is passed down to the next in line. My daughter was saying, "It's up to you Mom, to keep us all connected." From that conversation was born a "girls night out" in our family. This new tradition is now eight years old. We meet once a month. It consists of sisters-in-law, nieces and daughters. We go out to dinner, shopping, have game nights at our homes. The purpose is just to connect with each other on a regular basis in the midst of busy lives.

My husband comes from a family of 12 siblings. Most of them live in Minnesota. About a year after we had formed our girls' group here in Washington we went with two of our children to Minnesota to visit family. My daughter and I shared about our girls' night-out group and I jokingly said, "We should plan a girls' weekend once a year." Before we went back home to Washington we had a trip planned to Palm Springs the following spring. That was 7 years ago. And now our four-day trips have grown into 6 days. What I have found happens on these weekenders is that when you go to sleep in the same house with someone and wake up with them, there are all these blocks of time for getting to know each other better. Conversations go to a deeper level than when sitting around a dinner table with all of the family present. I watched our daughter's watching us moms laughing and being playful together. Often it's hard to separate who are the moms and who are the daughters. In the midst of these sister weekends we are teaching our daughters that age is only a number and youthfulness is a state of mind. We have special moments of conversation with each other's daughters, and with each other as sisters. We gather in the hot tub sharing stories with our daughters until 2am. We go home with memories we will carry with us for a lifetime.

I am also part of a women's dinner group. It began with a phone call from a friend one afternoon with an idea for this group. We each brought two friends to our first gathering. We have been together for 5 years. At least most of us have been. A few have come and gone. Sometimes as women we try people on and they don't fit for whatever reason. I find that is part of the process of creating life-long friends. We meet once a month in each other's homes or gather at a local restaurant. I find when you bring groups of people together, as they get to know each other they act a lot like family. As we have gotten to know each other we have experienced growing pains, just like in a family. But the longer we're together, the deeper the bonds grow. And I see lasting friendships developing.

As I sit here doing the final editing of this book I am reflecting on this years "sister trip" that I just recently returned home from. This year we gathered in Sonoma in the midst of California's beautiful wine country. We rented this cozy little home bursting with ambiance that was owned by the Sebastiani family, with their beautiful winery located right outside our front door.

My daughter Kym and I arrived early in the day, drove out to Sonoma and settled into the house. Then later that night headed back into San Francisco Airport to pick up the Minnesota girls. Our first few hours are always filled with lots of energy and catching up and then as we settle in with each other, conversations always move to a deeper level. These conversations took place sitting cross-legged on a bed together, curled up on a couch, or walking on the wharf in San Francisco. The best ones seemed to take place around the kitchen table in the morning with everyone in their pj's and as my one niece describes it, with bad bed hair. One of my sisters-in-law lost a young husband this past year. As we shared in her tears we also celebrated our niece's new little son that recently arrived from Guatemala. What I realized as I sat listening to the stories was that when one precious life is taken from us, God fills that empty hole with a new life. What I so appreciate about these sisters is that they dare to share real and honest, unedited feelings.

As we said our goodbyes and headed to our separate gates at the airport we were already looking forward to our rendezvous next fall. New York City here we come!

Kym and Tahnya
My daughters

SOLITUDE

Learn to get in touch with the silence within yourself and know that everything in this life has a purpose.

Elizabeth kubler-Ross

In the midst of my busy life I need pockets of solitude. A place that momentarily removes me from my responsibilities and availability to those closest to me. I find when I honor these moments of solitude I honor the person God created me to be.

It's in the quiet that our spirit speaks to us, that we give ourselves permission to visit our dreams.

Solitude takes creativity in the midst of family life. Closing a bathroom door, soaking in a tub of warm water by candlelight scented with lavender, soft music playing in the background. Reading my favorite book or magazine and knowing I don't have to be anything to anybody for 30 minutes. Taking a moonlit walk when the rest of the world is quiet and asleep. When we get really good at this, we may even go away for a weekend with a girlfriend.

As women we wear many hats. Among them, mother, wife, cook, taxi driver, decorator, maid, counselor, negotiator, friend and lover just to name a few. It's so easy to give up who we are to meet the needs of those around us. To always put ourselves at the bottom of the list and often we never reach the bottom of that list. Somewhere along the way we get sacrificed. If we don't take time for these moments of solitude we give ourselves away. We forget who we are and get lost in the process. I cherish all my roles, but I also want to honor the talents God placed in me and I want a part of me to be separate from the other titles I carry. I recently read in a book some advice mothers were passing on to their daughters. One mother said, "take care of yourself first so you can take care of your family."

Honoring our life and purpose. Renewing our physical and emotional strength. Finding inner peace in the quiet times. That's what takes place in solitude.

In solitude we give passionate attention to our lives, to our memories, to the details around us.
Virginia Woolf

A friend called one day and shared this story with me. She woke up and felt the need for solitude. After she sent her three kids off to school she hopped in her car and headed north into the mountains. She drove until she found a little stream by the side of the road. Pulled over, grabbed her writing tablet and found a big rock close to the water and perched on top of it. This is how she described her day. "The cool autumn breeze danced across my face and gently tugged at orange and gold leaves clinging to the almost bare trees that surrounded me. Fall was in the air and its smells and sounds nurtured my soul and gave me the sense of peace I was searching for earlier that morning. Sometimes life gets too busy and I just need to remove myself and find a quiet place." For her it is somewhere in nature. She's a writer. Writing for her is therapy. She said, "What I find in these times of solitude is discovering who I am and what's important to me. These times of solitude quiet my spirit and I find peace."

Another friend shared this story. It was 11pm. Restlessness had been her constant companion all day. On her way to her bedroom late that night she glanced out a window and noticed snow was lightly falling outside. Something stirred inside her and a whole new plan began developing. Her spirit was seeking adventure. She is married to an artist and does his marketing, sales and shipping from a home-based office and often feels cut off from the outside world. Her husband had recently bought her a new corvette convertible. Instead of going to bed that night, she packed a bag and headed out to her car. She crawled in behind the steering wheel, put the top down and drove to Vancouver, Canada to visit a close friend. She said it was the most exhilarating feeling as she sped up the freeway in the middle of the night. For a moment she had removed herself from her world of responsibilities and found solitude in the middle of the night where stars twinkled overhead and snowflakes melted on her face. For just a moment, the world was hers.

SANDRA J. GOOSELAW

From my journal

My Trip To The Beach
Poi Pou Beach, Kauaii

    I am drawn to the water in the early morning hours when the rest of the world is still quiet and asleep. I head out my front door with fins and snorkel in hand and take a left at the gate, crossing the park to the sandy beach that waits for me on the other side of the grassy field. The morning sun has already begun drying the dewy grass as my bare feet slide across it and smells of salt water greet me and begin waking my senses. Birds talk to each other overhead and I hear the clang of the garbage man up the street.

    *The sun is already warming my body as it hovers overhead, and my eyes wander out over the blue tropical waters hoping to catch sight of a ship passing by. The atmosphere that surrounds me embraces my early morning mood and nurtures my spirit. My imagination takes me to unknown worlds as I let it carry me to the other side of the ocean. In these early morning forays to the beach the world is mine for a brief moment. I embrace the smells, the sounds, and the quiet. As I slip into my fins and place the snorkel in my mouth I walk out into the water until it eventually picks me up and gently carries me across it and I enter a world of colorful creatures and for this moment "**the world is mine.**"*

COMFORTABLE IN MY OWN SHOES

I have found that most of us sometime in our life try to measure up to someone else's expectations of us. By nature we have the need to fit in, to be accepted. Sometimes we let others define and label who we are and we buy into that belief. Life became easier for me when I figured out what I required of myself. For me it began with finding a sense of comfort and peace within myself. I found when I grew into who I was meant to be; I became truly happy and content. I quit measuring myself by someone else's standards.

I think for each of us as women, we find our comfort zones. We all wear different hats because of our talents and gifts that we carry inside us. I don't believe for a minute that we were all meant to be stay-at-home moms. Would the world be a better place if we were? I don't know. Sometimes we are better mothers and wives because we do work outside our home. Today we have the choice. And it's not about the fact that we all have to do it the same way or it's bad. There's no one way to make it work for each of us as women. Hopefully we can honor the diversity in each other. I have never believed that being a stay at home mom is the only honorable thing to do.

For me, I knew the day I went back to work after our first daughter arrived that I didn't belong there anymore. But I also came home and created a business to do at home because I loved working. My belief is that whatever we decide to do, do it in a healthy way. If we go back to work, do it without guilt.

My twenties and thirties were all about designing my life, becoming a wife, mother, and stay at home mom. When I turned 40 it felt like coming home. And I think that is when I really began my journey of coming into the woman I have evolved into today.

We need to fall in love with ourselves. Love ourselves unconditionally. It doesn't make any difference if we're tall or short, thin or wide, because on the inside we are each *unique* and that's where our real beauty shines. Growing up with four brothers and their friends I was subjected to a lot of teasing, so I learned early on to not take life too seriously or personally. I also learned to laugh at myself. I grew up thinking my nose was too long, my chin too short, I was too tall, too thin and I get this little lisp when I get too tired. But then one day I grew into myself and just accepted it all. I realized all "that stuff" make's me who I am and I began embracing her. And then one day I fell in love with her and truly became "comfortable in my own shoes."

MARRIAGE

We are only as great as the people who surround us.

I love being married. They say marriage is a journey. We are two equals coming together as one. Who said that? Equal what? I remember when my husband and I were dating and he said to me, "Honey, I could *never* get mad at you." Today I wonder, *"Where did that man go?"* When we are first married we get lost in the *"wonder"* of it all and then some where along the way we move into the wonder of "what in the world was I thinking?" Why do some marriages work and others don't? We all begin with the same intent, don't we? Till death do us part. Somewhere along the way something changes. I believe often we aren't even aware of the changing that takes place in our every day living, until one day we wake up and no longer recognize the person lying next to us. We find ourselves wondering, "Who is this man, and where did he come from?"

I believe marriage *is* about coming together as equals and growing together. Some couples don't come into it believing that or treat each other less than equal and grow into that belief. I think that can go either way.

Sometimes as women we are equally guilty of treating men as less than equal. Or maybe it's because men are from Mars and women are from Venus and we came together on planet Earth without an instruction book. Assumptions, lack of communication, unrealistic expectations often destroy that romantic love that brought us together.

For me, marriage is about loving this man I married, just as he is, and feeling equally loved in return. I want to be loved and honored for who I am and I want to give that same respect back to him. I want him to be my best friend and I want to be his. I want to be that someone he can't wait to come home to at night because he knows I'm there waiting for him. I want him to know without a doubt how much he is loved and cherished.

Like any journey, there are the hills and valleys and ruts in the road. Sometimes we feel like we get lost along the way. And isn't it funny how the things that were *so* cute to us before we married this guy, quickly become *so* irritating after we say I do. What do you suppose clouds our vision?

Our best talks take place sitting cross-legged on the floor facing each other. He's not only my friend, he's my soulmate. I honor my position as his wife and never take my role lightly. What makes it work for us?? We both have kept that little child alive in us and always keep him close to the surface. We like each other. Liking is so much different than loving. We listen when the other speaks and we honor each other for who we are individually and don't try and change that person. And we laugh at each other. A lot!!

Marriage *is* a journey and like any journey there are always the unexpected turns in the road, the bumps that seem to knock us off our feet for a while. But I have found when I get to the other side of the bump I am stronger, and when I willingly follow that turn in the road there is that unexpected surprise waiting for me. What I have found is that after I make my "well made plans" and then turn them over to God, He takes all the kinks out and makes them more perfect than I ever could have dreamed they could be.

SOME DAYS YOU JUST GOTTA DANCE!!

It was a warm summer evening and my husband and I were dining at a restaurant on the water. As we left the restaurant and walked outside music was filling the air and I looked over my shoulder at him and said, "Shall we dance?" Jokingly, of course. He immediately pulled me into his arms and started dancing me around the outside deck. As he whirled me around my eyes took in the restaurant windows facing us and a lot of eyeballs were focused on us. I said to him, "Don't look now, but it feels like the whole restaurant is watching us." He smiled at me and said, "It's ok! More people need to dance."

We often hold ourselves in such rigid and restrained behaviors because we feel it's so much more acceptable to those in the world watching us. When everything inside of us is screaming to live life just a little bit braver and a little bit louder. Growing up with 4 brothers I think I was forced to live life a little braver. I also had a playful dad and the day I was born part of his spirit was born in mine. I'm so thankful for that. He taught me how to "dance" and live life large.

I love the hearts of kids because they live life unedited. And they see life with fresh eyes and this huge imagination. Tears and smiles are a part of their day and if they feel like twirling, they twirl. We all need to twirl more.

I keep my inner child close to the surface, and if for a time I have to put him away, I know he's always there for easy access. I chose to live in awe of each new day and know that it's a gift to be treasured.

I challenge each of you to find the child that's buried deep within you, because we all have one. And let's just dance!

To my readers,

Thank you for coming along on this incredible journey with me. During these past few months of writing and taking time to notice the rich details in the friendships that fill my life, I feel a new appreciation for each woman whose story I share. I hope somewhere in these stories, something has touched your life. I challenge each woman who reads this book to *dare to be different*. To walk away from gossip. To be the person God created you to be. To be genuine in all your relationships and to live each day with purpose. You will be amazed at the changes that will occur in your life and the new relationships and events that show up. We receive from the world what we give to the world. Our happiness is never something we get from other people. We first find it inside ourselves and then what we give to the world is returned to us.

What did I realize at the end of my project?

I think I have a diamond necklace!!

I would like to leave you with this poem I wrote many years ago that speaks about opportunity and how high we dare soar.

Anything is possible
If we only try_
God gives us the courage and wisdom
It's up to *us how high we fly*.
Life's just like the patches on a quilt. It's up to us to pick the pieces we put into it and how colorful we make it.

Blessings,
Sandy

Nothing can bring you peace but yourself."

Ralph Waldo Emerson